Snow Leopard

Children Book of Fun Facts & Amazing Photos on Animals in Nature - A Wonderful Snow Leopard Book for Kids aged 3-7

By

Ina Felix

Ina Felix

Copyright © 2015 by Ina Felix

All rights reserved. No part of this book may be used or reproduced in any manner whatsoever without the express written permission of the publisher except for the use of brief quotations in a book review. Image Credits: Royalty free images reproduced under license from various stock image repositories. Under a creative commons licenses.

I am a snow leopard.

I am a big cat but still smaller than lions and tigers.

I have quite a short body; my legs are also quite short.

I always keep my body strong and healthy.

I have a very long tail.

Unlike other cats, my eyes can be green or grey.

My thick fur, as white as the snow, is spotted with black dots.

I can be found all over the southeastern part of the world.

I can be very hard to find because my family and I are rare.

I do not have a lot of relatives like other animals.

I am able to live and stay in mountains with very cold weather.

My paws are wide, so it makes walking on snow easier for me.

I love travelling around places alone.

When I give birth to cubs, I stay with them until they grow older.

In the mountains, I train my cubs to fight for themselves.

When the sun rises, I feel so energetic.

When the sun sets, my energy still remains.

Meat is my favorite food.

I can hunt for bad animals that are a lot larger than me.

Even if I like being alone, I don't leave my buddy behind.

I hope you had fun learning about my family.

Thank you.

Made in the USA
Lexington, KY
08 May 2017